Are We On The Same Page?

A poetic story of him & her...

Tejaswini Sawant Dak

BookLeaf Publishing

India | USA | UK

Made with ❤ on the BookLeaf Publishing Platform
www.bookleafpub.in
www.bookleafpub.com

Dedication

To my soulmate Digvijay Dak,

Our marriage was arranged by our families. In arranged marriages, families often introduce potential partners to their children, encouraging them to consider these options and assess compatibility for a lifelong commitment.

Before meeting a potential match, individuals may experience a range of emotions, including curiosity, nervousness, pressure, and excitement.

The success of an arranged marriage depends on various factors, such as open communication, mutual respect, shared goals, and family support.

While it's possible for people to fall in love after getting married in an arranged setting, love can develop over time as couples get to know each other and build a connection.

After enjoying eight years of successful married life, I decided to pen down our story.

These words trace the path of our love, from our first meeting to our decision to spend our lives together. Each poem is a reflection of the journey we have shared and shows the way we unleashed the layers of our emotions since we met.

Preface

In this collection, Tejaswini invites us to immerse ourselves in a poetic love story that resonates with every him and her who has ever fallen in love.

As an architect by profession, she has always had a keen eye for design and structure. But in these verses, she reveals a different kind of blueprint—one that maps the twists and turns of love, curiosity, confusion and longing.

With a poet's sensitivity and a lover's heart, Tejaswini explores the highs and lows of human connection.

From the phase of searching for a right match to the decision of spending the entire life together her words capture the full spectrum of emotions and tell you a story of those two familiar strangers who get introduced by their families in the process of arranged marriage.

As a woman who has embraced creativity in all its forms,
She brings a unique perspective to her exploration of
love.

She loves singing, dancing and runs a YouTube channel
'Tej Diaries' with her husband Digvijay.

Whether you are a seasoned lover or just beginning to
explore the complexities of romance, this collection will
show you the depth and richness that resonates on a
personal level.

Acknowledgements

I would like to express my deepest gratitude to my beloved husband, Digvijay, for being the perfect match in my life. Eight years of marriage have flown by, filled with both joy and challenges. Through it all, he has been my constant support, my biggest cheerleader, and my best friend.

I am eternally grateful for the encouragement and support he has given me. His unwavering belief in me has helped me overcome obstacles and achieve my goals. I am so thankful for our relationship and for the way we have grown together.

To my amazing parents, I extend my heartfelt thanks for the friendly and modern upbringing they provided. They allowed me to explore my own boundaries and make my own decisions, which has instilled in me a sense of independence and confidence. Your trust in me has meant the world. Knowing that you believe in my abilities has given me the courage to pursue my dreams. Thank you for always being there for me.

I would also like to express my sincere gratitude to all my friends and family for sharing your life stories with me. Your experiences have been a source of inspiration and wisdom. When I start writing, I often find myself reflecting on the stories you've shared and drawing parallels to my own life.

A huge shoutout to my best friend, Shweta Dabetwar, for being an incredible support system while writing this book. Her insights and encouragement were invaluable. Thank you so much for everything!

I am truly blessed to have you all in my life. Your love, support, and friendship have made this journey possible. Thank you.

1. A Glimpse Of An Unclear Face

His Feelings, When in search of love:

A face unclear, a distant call,
A mind entangled, finding its fall...

Behind the eyes, a silent gaze,
Stealing thoughts in subtle ways...
A whiff of scent, a silent plea,
A reflection deep within, you see...

In twilight's hush, a gentle sigh,
A fleeting touch, I can't deny...
A soul to connect, I yearn to find,
Peace of mind, a friend so kind...

To share my joys, my sorrows deep,
With someone I can truly keep...
To laugh and cry, to fight and mend,
A bond unbreakable, till the end...

To find a love that's pure and true,
A heart that beats in rhythm with you...
To hold your hand, through thick and thin,
To face the world, and always win...

A love so strong, it knows no fear,
A love that's constant, year by year...
In every glance, a story told,
A thought so deep, a love to unfold...

A heart that yearns, a soul that's free,
To find a love that's meant to be...
A face unclear, a distant call,
A mind entangled, finding its fall...

2. A Lonely Night

Her Feelings, When in search of love:

Alone I stand,
beneath the moonlit sky,
Awaiting someone,
I don't know why...

My heart yearns
for a compatible soul,
To fill the void,
to make me whole...

Lost in thoughts, I ponder deep,
Who will come, my heart to keep?
A gentle breeze, a soothing touch,
A moment's peace, I long for such...

In quiet dreams,
a mystery face,
A smile that fills
this lonely space...

Together we wander,
hand in hand,
Through fields of green,
across the land...

A love so pure,
a bond so true,
A shining world of
me and you...

So let us hope,
and wait with grace,
For love to find
its rightful place...

3. Heartbeats Of A Dreaming Heart

\# Her Feelings, When in search of love:

With my eyes wet,
In the dark...
My faith yearns heartbeats,
Of a dreaming heart...

You must be feeling
Me somewhere...
With twinkling light,
And deep heart care...

Come soon darling,
In my life...
Like soft dark touch
Of blue moon light...
Let me feel the ocean of love,
Beyond the line of my eyesight...

Come close,
Till I breathe so high...
Don't let our fingers,
get untied...
Make me fall
for you my pie...
I am dying to share
That breath I desire!

4. The Rhythm Of My Heartbeat Is Going To Change

\# His Feelings, When in search of love:

A canvas painted
with dreams of you,
A heart that's waited,
patient and true...
I yearn for love, A burning fire,
A maze of pain, a sweet desire...

Your time, your touch,
I long to claim,
A love so pure,
A golden flame...
As you enter my world,
Like a morning dew,
My heartbeat's rhythm,
Would be a melody new...

5. Awaiting Your Love

Her Feelings, When in search of love:

Have you ever
seen my eyes,
Yearning for your
presence wise...
Have you ever
seen me in the crowd,
Lost in thoughts,
feeling so profound?

I've searched for you,
in every way...
Hoping you'd
Come to stay...
A caring soulmate,
a precious prize,
I dream of you,
when the mornings rise...

I crave your presence,
near and dear,
To chase away
the doubts and fear...
I long to know
the feelings true,
That fill your heart,
With me and you...

Life has a lot of
twists and turns,
I am Lost in the storm,
where the wild mind runs...
I wait for you,
my love, my all,
To answer my
silent and heartfelt call...

6. A Mind At Play

When they get introduced by family:

Thoughts dance and swirl,
a dizzying play,
A mind adrift,
lost in its own way...

Questions and doubts,
they fill the air,
As curiosity takes hold,
Unaware...

A familiar stranger, a puzzle untold,
A connection deep, a story to unfold...

The heart yearns,
a mystery to solve,
As the mind wanders,
lost and involved...

7. A Twist Of Fate

\# When they get introduced by family:

We met by chance,
a twist of fate,
Still need some time,
but this phase seems great...

Our friendship bloomed,
deep and true,
A connection unlike
any other knew...

Trust and faith, a sacred tie,
A bond so strong, a reason why...

Your presence fills
my soul with light,
Guiding me
through the darkest night...

But is this bond,
so strong and deep,
A fleeting moment
or a dream to keep?

Is life so simple,
a carefree game?
Will this bond last,
forever the same?

I wonder
if this trust we share,
Is real and true,
beyond compare...
Or is it just
a passing phase,
A mirage
in life's endless maze?

I hope it's more,
a lasting grace,
A love that time
cannot erase...

8. A Change Of Heart

\# When they get introduced by family:

Since I've known you,
my life has changed,
A newfound passion,
A love unarranged...

My thoughts, my feelings,
now intertwined,
A connection deep,
of heart and mind...

My heart once peaceful,
now feels a stir,
A longing, a yearning,
I can't ignore...

Your presence feels, like a candle light,
A warmth that pampers me, through the night...

Though words may fail,
my heart does speak...
A silent message,
Your heart foreseek...

I hope you'll hear it,
loud and clear...
Secretly you know about
the love I hold so dear...

Doubts may linger,
Like shadows of night...
But faith says,
Future with you looks bright...

A flame that burns,
A passion that's true...
A love for you,
Seems forever new...

9. A Heart Entangled

When they get curious and confused about their
feelings:

Looping thoughts,
And a curious mind..
A heart unfulfilled,
left behind...

Memories linger,
The uncertain mess,
Is this love unspoken?
Still finding embrace...

Settlement of expectations,
Hoping for good luck...
Feeling confused at some point,
Are we emotionally stuck?

A Promise to keep,
a dream deferred,
This journey of love story,
still seems so blurred...

With passing time,
the fog will lift...
Confusion's grip,
will slowly shift...

A newfound curiosity,
will take its place...
As hearts connect,
in a warm embrace...

10. A Heart's Desire

\# When they get curious and confused about their
feelings:

Like a dancing kite,
in the wind,
Lost in thoughts,
I wander blind...

With every breath,
a new desire,
A longing deep,
a burning fire...

Your words feel like,
A gentle breeze,
They Whisper secrets,
Keeping mind at ease...

My eyes, like butterflies,
flutter and play...
Lost in the beauty of
a shining day...

The fragrance of wet earth,
Is like gentle touch,
Your presence is what,
I cherish so much...

A bond so strong,
a trust so deep,
Love is a sweet nectar,
A treasure to keep...

With you by my side,
I'm never alone,
Your love feels pure,
That brought me ashore...

11. A Heart Unfulfilled

When they get curious and confused about their feelings:

Words entangled,
feelings entwined,
Love is still incomplete,
It's game of mind...

Who should I blame,
who should I praise,
Lost in thoughts,
a maze of ways...

Your absence in life,
Echoes a constant pain,
Tears get collected,
like drops of rain...

You visit me in dreams,
a fleeting sight,
Igniting hope,
a guiding light...

Love still feels like,
a broken part,
Without you by my side,
my aching heart...

12. A Poem Of Hope And Love

\# When unknowingly hearts connect:

In life's journey,
ups and downs abound,
Like shadows dancing,
and number of faces around...

What is friendship & what is love,
we must discern,
While in search of a soulmate,
we must learn...

In the depths of hearts,
a bond is tied,
By fate's design,
it's an emotional ride...

Though lonely now,
someone will come,
To fill your life
With love to blossom...

With dreams of love,
painted in the mind,
Each heart yearns,
A soulmate to find...

Though mistakes may come,
let's not despair,
It's time to grow
With hope and care...

So let's embrace the future,
with hearts aglow,
For love to find its way,
we'll surely know...

13. If Only He Could

When unknowingly hearts connect:

If only he could
understand,
The dreams I hold,
within my hand...
The love I yearn for,
pure and true,
A love like his,
just me and you...

If only he could
feel the spark,
That ignites my heart,
night and dark...
The longing echoes,
a constant plea,
For him to be
the one for me...

If only he could
see my dream,
My destiny
Pulling me to him..
The love we'd share,
a perfect pair,
A bond so strong,
Beyond compare...

If only he could
paint the future,
A world of love,
without a suture...
A life together,
hand in hand,
A peaceful mind,
And golden sand...

If only he could
see the love,
A secret whisper,
A silent dove..
To hear my heart's plea,
a silent refrain,
Be mine forever,
And ease my pain...

14. With You By My Side

\# When unknowingly hearts connect:

With you by my side,
my love will bloom,
A bond so strong,
defying time's gloom...

A seed of friendship,
a love to grow,
A feeling so pure,
For hearts to glow...

If trust is the guide,
We can find our way,
Through life's challenges,
come what may...

Together we'll dream,
our dreams we'll share,
And build a future,
beyond compare...

Your love will light
my path, so bright,
Dispelling darkness,
And crossing all the height...

Hand in hand,
We will start this ride...
It's time for you,
To stand by my side...

15. What Is Love?

\# When unknowingly hearts connect:

Love's a gentle breeze,
a soothing sigh,
Whispering secrets,
to the open sky...

A beacon shining,
in the darkest night,
Filling souls with hope,
so pure and bright...

Love's a tender touch,
a warm embrace,
Comforting the soul,
in life's vast space...

A melody of joy,
a sweet refrain,
Erasing sorrow,
and easing pain...

Love's a power,
a guiding hand,
Leading hearts
across the land...

Love's a shared journey,
a path unknown,
A story to be written,
A zone of our own...

16. Just You & Me

When they start missing each other:

At this very moment,
I miss to be with you...
If wind allows me,
I may fly to you...

Feeling distant,
far apart,
I wish to turn
and mend my heart...

Talking, talking,
endless flow,
I'd love for this
to never go...
Lost in thought,
so deeply drowned,
I want to forget
what's around...

Just you and me,
no one else,
Beneath the stars,
our love excels...
Drifting away,
so free and light,
In this moment,
all feels just right...

17. Memory's A Mirage

When they start missing each other:

What is a memory,
you ask..
A mirage, a thirst, a task...

A forgotten dream,
A hazy scene,
Sometimes a wish,
And a hope serene...

It's a painted dream, a vivid art,
Or a longing, for a brand new start...

Some thoughts dancing, Just wild and free..
A faded hue, A mind mystery...

A memory is a fleeting thought,
A heartfelt moment dearly brought...

18. A Dream Of Union

When they start missing each other:

A longing deep within my soul,
To find a love that makes me whole...

To feel your touch, your gentle kiss,
A miracle of love, a moment of bliss...

To lose myself, to find us two,
In love's embrace, forever new...

A moment pure, a perfect state,
Where hearts entwined,
and souls integrate...

A dream I hold, a hope I keep,
To find in you, a love so deep...

To merge with you, a perfect blend,
A love that knows no earthly end...

19. An Emotional Storm

When they start missing each other:

I still long,
to know you,
To understand you
deeply and true...

To comprehend
your feelings' hue,
And calm the emotional
storm within you...

To find my happiness
in your smile,
And wipe away
each tear awhile...

To shelter you
from every storm,
To mend your heart,
and keep it calm...

To accept you,
just as you are,
A shining star,
So bright and far...

To be the reason
of your spark,
Your guiding light,
your beacon stark...

20. When It Rains

When they fall in love:

When it rains,
It's a gentle caress on her cheeks
Each drop is a memory,
A moment frozen in time...

When it rains,
Her laughter is a melody,
Feels like a symphony of joy...
Her eyes, mirrors of her soul,
Reflecting love's divine light...

When it rains,
Their hands, entwined,
It's a silent promise, unspoken...
Their hearts, beating as one,
In a world of their own...

When it rains,
There is a stolen kiss,
A whispered secret,
Their souls find solace,
A love so pure, to embrace...

When it rains,
In a quiet night,
A sparkling love finds a connection...
A deep affection,
Shining silver & bright,
The unrestrained wave of attraction...

21. I Want To Be The Rain

\# When they fall in love:

I want to be the rain,
A gentle fall,
To drench the earth,
to answer the call..
I will break my rhythm,
like a surprise gift,
I will cleanse your soul,
And make it complete...

I want to be the rain,
In those misty mornings,
on a hill so high,
Where hearts go fly...
No need to part,
this warmth, this bliss,
To feel your touch,
a tender kiss...

I want to be the rain,
To rinse away your fears...
To dissolve myself,
In your secret salty tears...
I'll be your comfort,
your constant friend,
A love that has
no sight of end...

22. Epilogue: A New Beginning

When they fall in love:

Now life seems to be,
Well aligned...
Our lips get locked,
And hearts entwined,
No longer lost,
We've found our way,
Together we'll face
each coming day...

Each touch, a spark,
A burning desire,
Melting us both
with a fiery fire...
It's feeling like a new world,
A vast and open sea,
To explore together,
Being wild and free...

Your touch, a flame,
Ignites my soul,
Your love & care,
Makes me feel whole..
We are thrilled to conquer,
All the couple goals set,
United forever,
Until the last breath...